BOOK • VIDEO

HOT LICKS

JOE PASS
SOLO JAZZ GUITAR

C000224856

CONTENTS

To access video visit:
www.halleonard.com/mylibrary
Enter Code
5795-0623-0836-3062

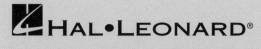

ISBN: 978-1-5400-8989-2

HAL•LEONARD®

Visit Hal Leonard Online at
www.halleonard.com

Contact us:
Hal Leonard
7777 West Bluemound Road
Milwaukee, WI 53213
Email: info@halleonard.com

In Europe, contact:
Hal Leonard Europe Limited
42 Wigmore Street
Marylebone, London, W1U 2RN
Email: info@halleonardeurope.com

In Australia, contact:
Hal Leonard Australia Pty. Ltd.
4 Lentara Court
Cheltenham, Victoria, 3192 Australia
Email: info@halleonard.com.au

BIOGRAPHY

Born Joseph Anthony Jacobi Passalaqua in 1929 in New Jersey, Joe Pass was both the apotheosis of the bop guitar tradition and an innovator who perfected a solo guitar style that turned the instrument into a self-sufficient band.

One of the latest-blooming jazz giants, Pass began recording the albums that set the standards for technical fluency well after he turned 40.

Pass became a professional while still in high school, playing in various swing bands, including a stint with Tony Pastor. He toured with band leader Charlie Barnet in 1947, but after a tour of duty in the military, he didn't return to the scene until the early 1960s.

Despite his late start, Pass quickly rose to the level of his idols Charlie Christian and Django Reinhardt. He eventually settled in Los Angeles and began making a name for himself with a series of recordings for Pacific Jazz, including 1963's *For Django*.

Pass spent the next decade playing local gigs, performing with Gerald Wilson, Les Mc-Cann, and George Shearing, and touring with Benny Goodman in 1973. That was the year Norman Granz signed him to Pablo, the famed jazz label that released Pass's legendary album *Virtuoso*—a landmark solo recording that has lost none of its potency over time.

During the next two decades, Pass recorded prolifically for Pablo, including sessions with Ella Fitzgerald, Oscar Peterson, Dizzy Gillespie, Milt Jackson, Duke Ellington, and Count Basie, as well as numerous albums of his own.

Pass remained active in both recording and performing, including an extensive tour with Guitar Summit, which also featured Paco Peña, Pepe Romero, and Leo Kottke.

Pass died of liver cancer in 1994, at the age of 65.

SELECT DISCOGRAPHY

For Django (Pacific Jazz, 1963)

Virtuoso (Pablo, 1973)

Portraits of Duke Ellington (Pablo, 1974)

Virtuoso #2 (Pablo, 1977)

Chops (Pablo, 1978)

I Remember Charlie Parker (Pablo, 1979)

Ira, George and Joe (Pablo, 1981)

We'll Be Together Again (Pablo, 1983)

Blues For Fred (Pablo, 1988)

One For My Baby (Pablo, 1989)

Appassionato (Pablo, 1990)

Virtuoso Live! (Pablo, 1991)

Virtuoso #3 (Pablo, 1992)

Virtuoso #4 (Pablo, 1993)

My Song (Telarc, 1993)

Joe Pass Quartet Live at Yoshi's (Pablo, 1993)

Duets (Pablo, 1996)

The Best of Joe Pass (Pacific Jazz, 1997)

Guitar Virtuoso (Pablo, 1997)

SUGGESTED LISTENING

Count Basie *April in Paris* (Verve, 1956)

Duke Ellington *Uptown* (Columbia, 1952)

Charlie Christian *The Genius of the Electric Guitar* (Columbia, 1987); *Swing to Bop* (Natasha, 1993)

Wes Montgomery *Far Wes* (Pacific Jazz, 1958); *The Incredible Jazz Guitar of Wes Montgomery* (Riverside, 1960)

Jack Wilkins *The Jack Wilkins Quartet/You Can't Live Without It* (Chiaroscuro, 1977)

Joe Pass *For Django* (Pacific Jazz, 1963); *Virtuoso* (Pablo, 1973); *Virtuoso #2* (Pablo, 1977)

Chapter 1: Coloring the I-vi-ii-V

Example 1   Here are the basic changes with color tones
(:21)

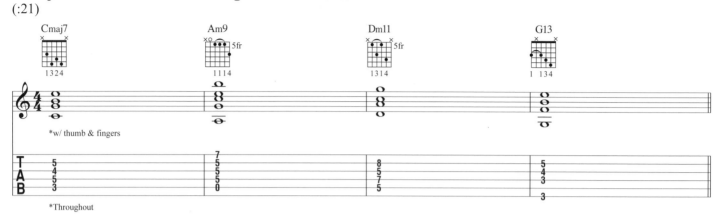

*w/ thumb & fingers

*Throughout

Example 2   Dominant 7 alterations
(1:22)

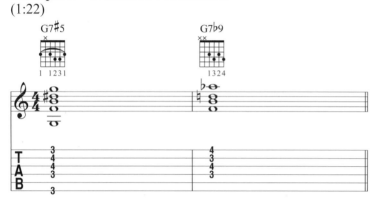

Example 3   The progression
(2:48)

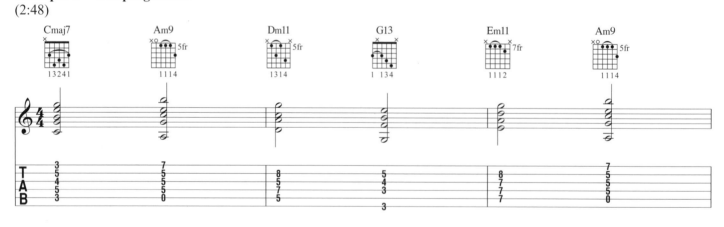

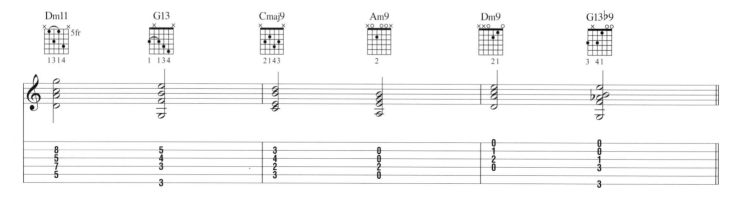

Example 4   Substitute A dominant 7th for A minor 7th
(3:30)

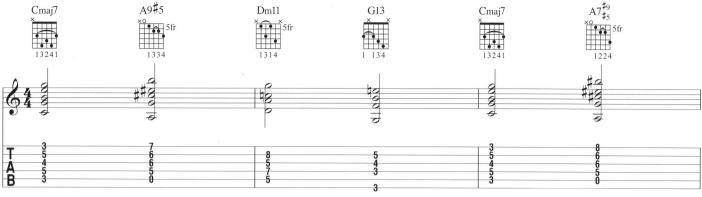

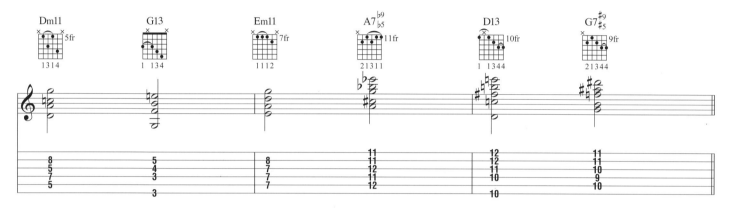

Example 5   Variations for A7
(3:54)

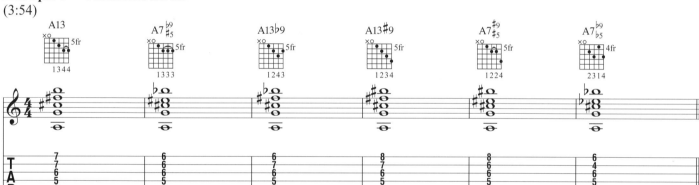

Example 6   Substitute D7 for Dm7
(4:49)

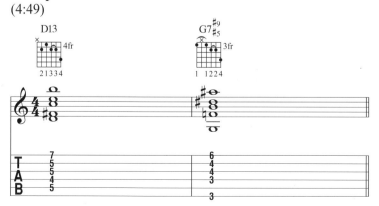

Example 7   Substitute Em for C major
(5:25)

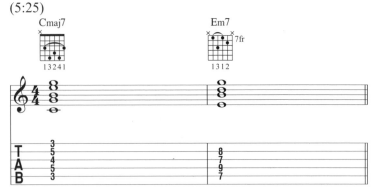

Example 8   Substitute Em or E7♯9 for C major
(5:53)

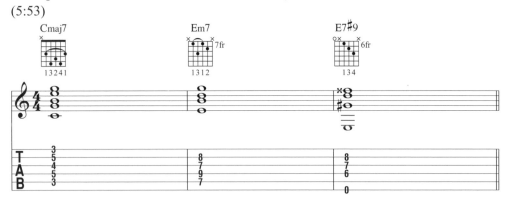

Example 9   Substitutions in a line – E7♯9 for C, A13 for Am, D7♯9 for Dm7
(6:50)

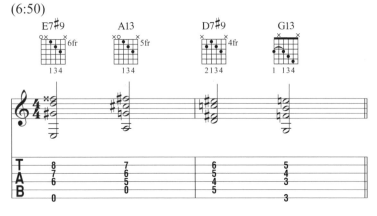

Example 10   Basic changes
(6:56)

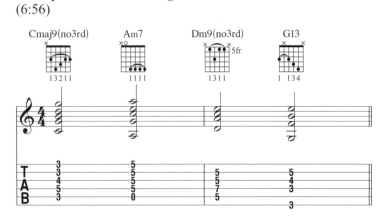

Example 11   Add tones to the substitutions
(7:15)

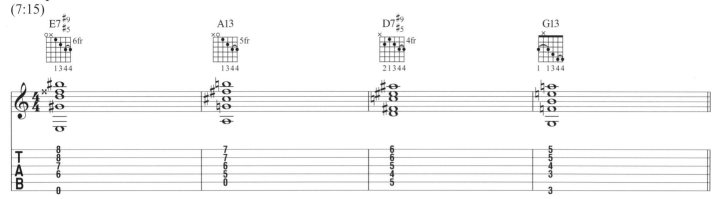

Example 12   Substitute B♭13 for E7♯9, A13 for E♭7♯9
(7:40)

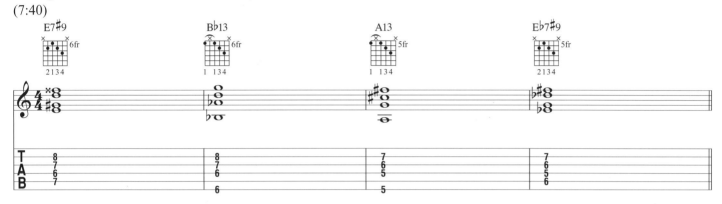

Example 13   Moving chromatically - B♭ for E, A♭7 for D
(9:03)

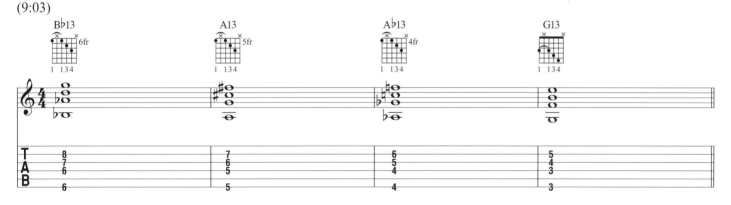

Example 14   Substitute E♭7 for A7, D♭7 for G7
(9:14)

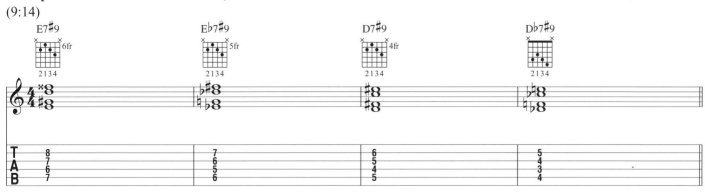

Example 15   Substitution recap
(9:22)

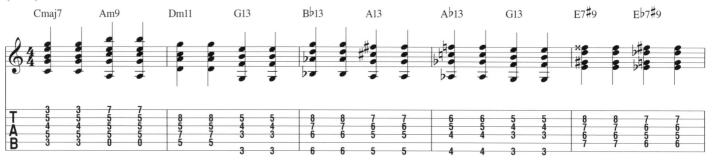

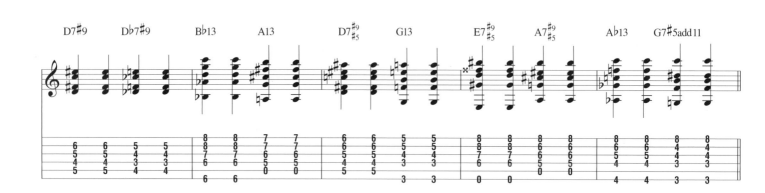

Example 16   Common tone – G on top
(10:40)

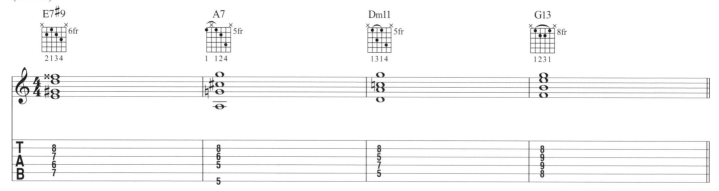

Example 17   Common tone – C on top
(10:51)

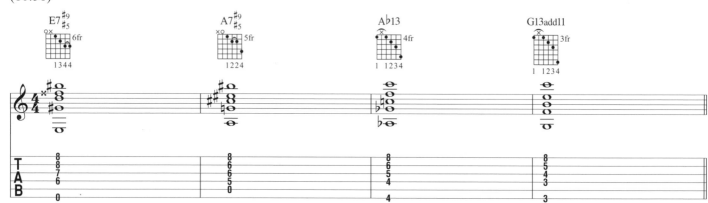

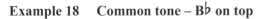

Example 18   Common tone – B♭ on top
(11:01)

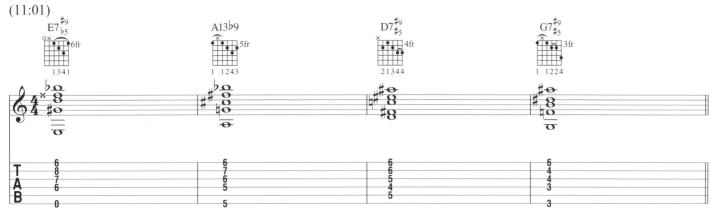

Example 19   Moving through the changes
(11:21)

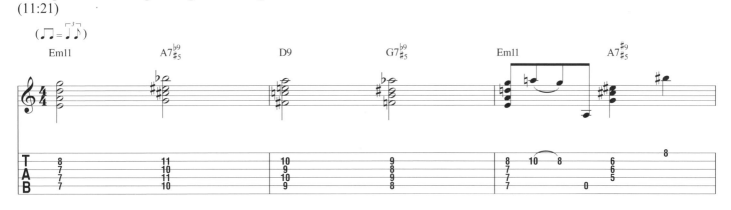

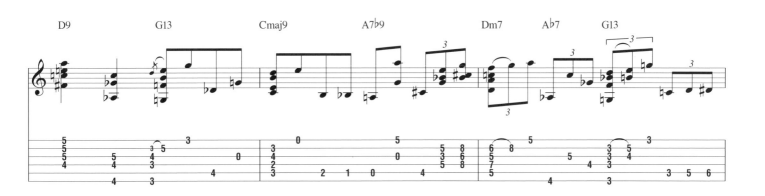

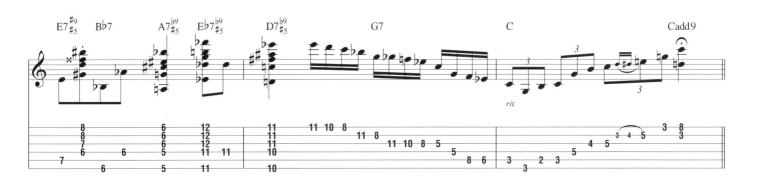

Chapter 2: Strategic Alterations

Example 20   Substitue E7♯9 for Cmaj7
(1:02)

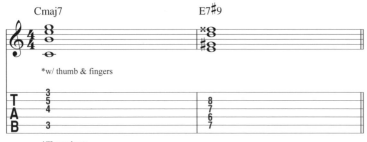

*w/ thumb & fingers

*Throughout

Example 21   Alterations should be on the top three strings
(2:28)   (2:48)

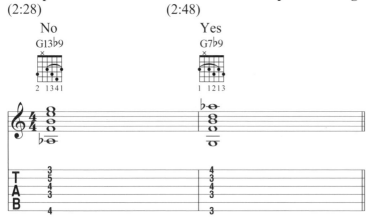

Chapter 3: More I-vi-ii-V Ideas

Example 22   Basic progression
(0:02)

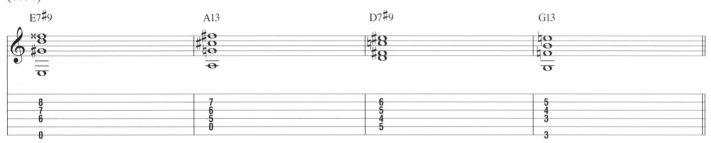

Substitute E7♯9 for Cmaj7
(0:04)

Chromatic substitutions
(0:14)

Example 23   Another substitution combination
(0:37)

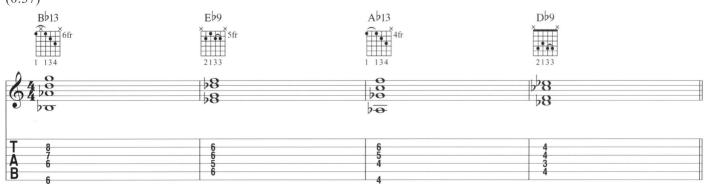

Example 24   I-vi-ii-V substitution solo
(0:52)

Example 25   Moving chromatically from I to vi
(1:19)

Example 26   Substitute B♭m7 for E7
(1:56)

Example 27   Substitute A♭m7 to D♭7 for G7
(3:22)

Example 28   A♭m is the ii, and D♭ is the ♭5 of G
(3:28)

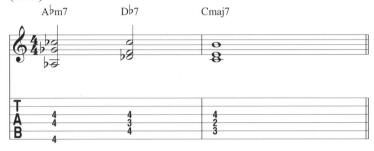

Example 29   Another option
(3:35)

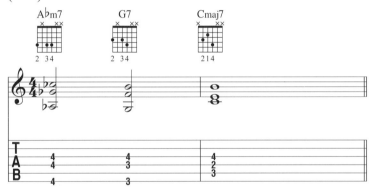

Example 30   Similar chord forms moved chromatically
(3:59)

Example 31   Little 3-note chords work the best (I -vi-ii-V)
(4:54)

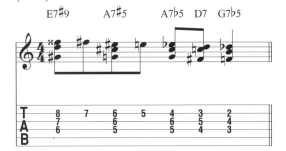

Example 32   Two notes for many situations in the key of C
(5:03)

Example 33   Some of the chord options that utilize D and G notes
(5:20)

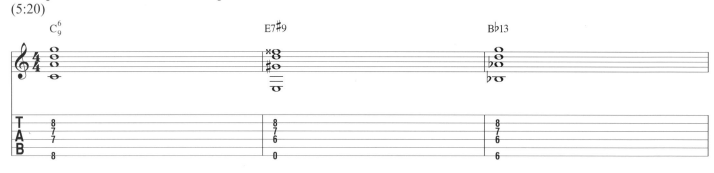

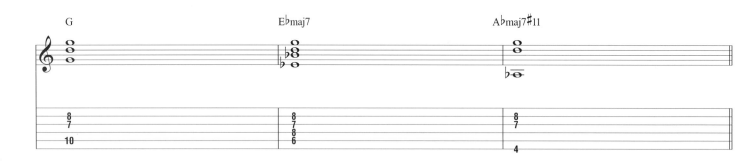

Chapter 4: Turnarounds

Example 34   Piano players' style of turnaround
(:22)

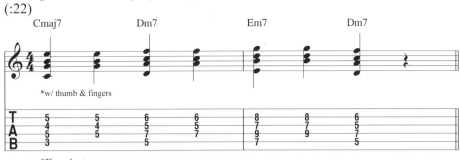

Example 35A   ii-V turnaround
(1:04)

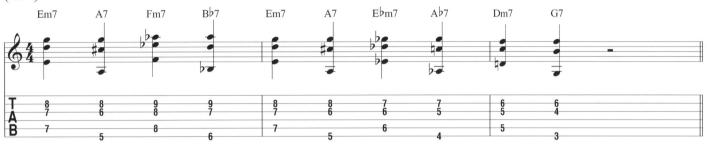

Example 35B   ii-V turnaround variation
(1:12)

Example 35C   I-vi-ii-V substition turnaround
(1:17)

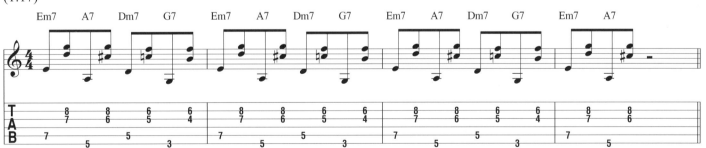

Example 35D   I-vi-ii-V related variation
(1:26)

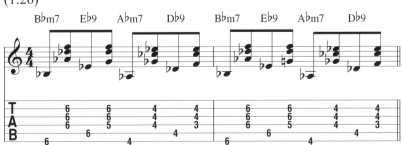

Chapter 5: Melodic Substitutions

Example 36   Basic I-vi-ii-V single-note line
(:20)

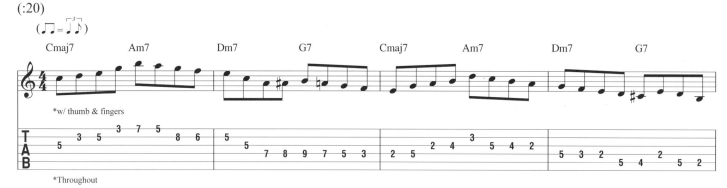

*w/ thumb & fingers

*Throughout

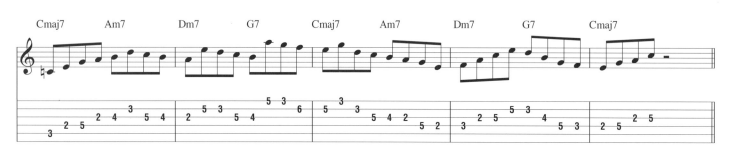

Example 37   Substitution chords enhance your melodic lines
(:40)

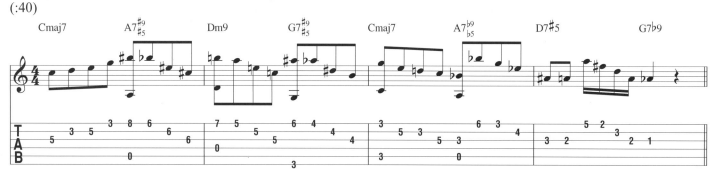

Example 38   I-vi
(:50)

Example 39   ii
(:59)

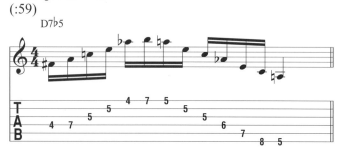

Example 40   V-I
(1:05)

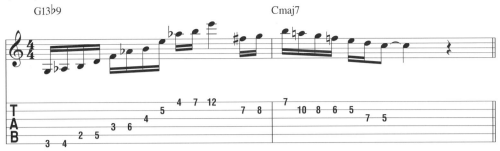

Example 41   Sample single-note line
(1:11)

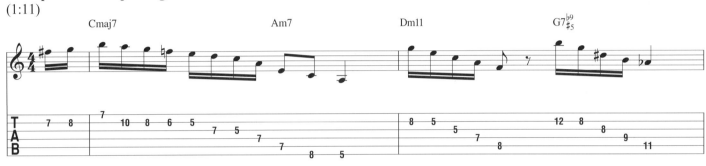

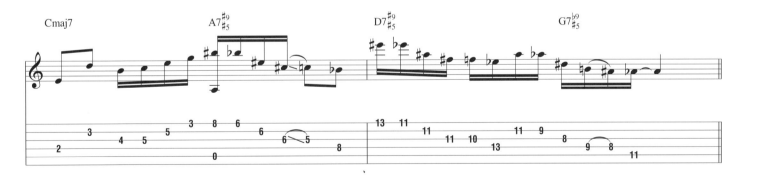

Example 42   I-vi-ii-V with substitutions
(1:38)

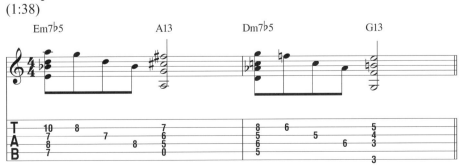

Example 43   More options
(1:46)

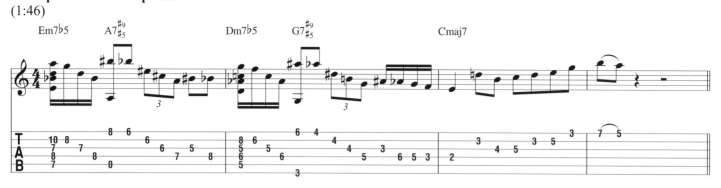

Example 44   Single line improv on I-vi-ii-V – basic to more complex
(2:12)

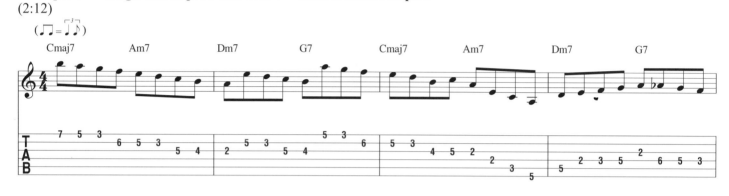

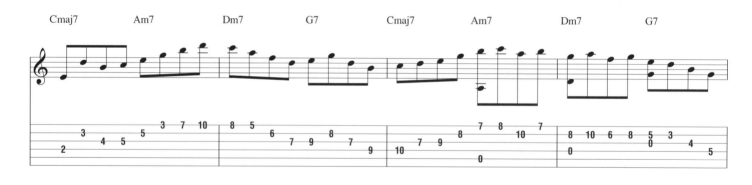

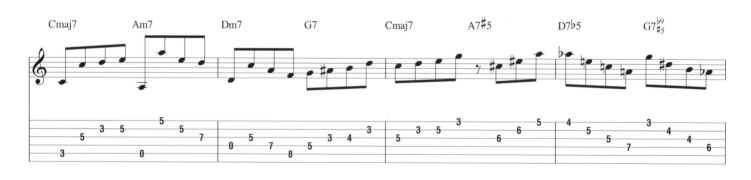

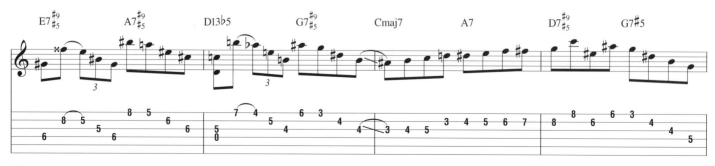

Example 45   Descending chromatically
(3:22)

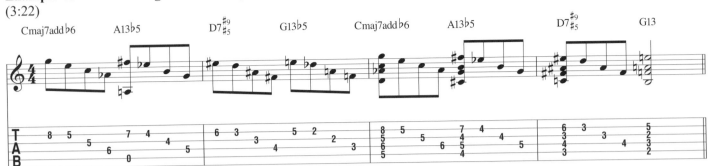

Example 46A   I
(3:40)

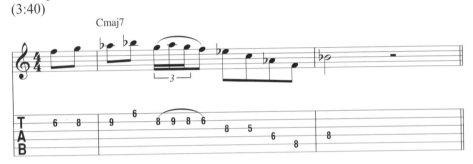

Example 46B   vi
(3:45)

Example 46C   ii
(3:48)

Example 46D   V
(3:51)

Example 47   Sample solo with substitutions
(3:54)

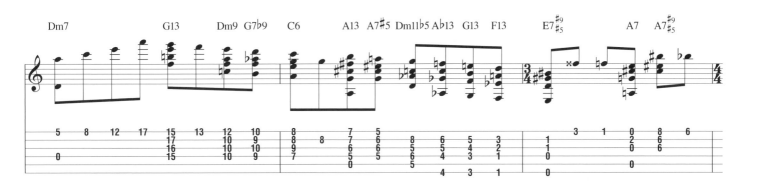

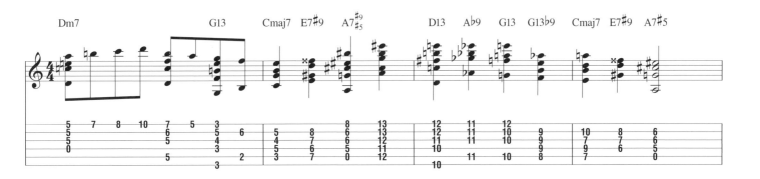

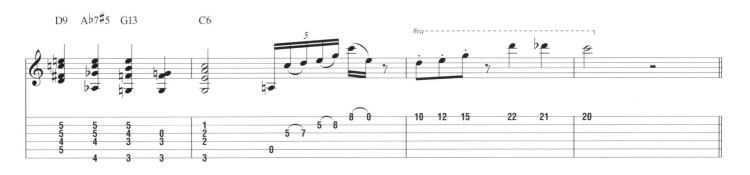

Chapter 6: Modes and Chord Scales -
How to Practice Scales in a Meaningful Way

Example 48   High B♭ note, with a chord below
(1:06)

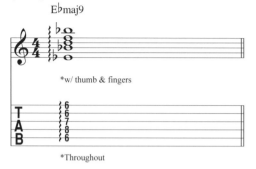

Example 49   Scale from the root to the top note of the chord
(1:28)

Example 50   Another chord with the same top note
(2:04)

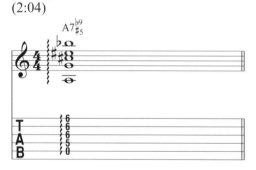

Example 51   Scale fro the root to the high B♭
(2:17)

Example 52   Another chord with the same top note
(2:30)

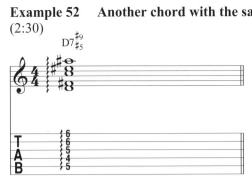

Example 53
(2:40)

Example 54
(4:11)

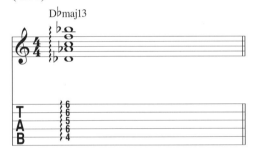

Example 55
(4:39)

Example 56A
(4:44)

Example 56B
(4:48)

Example 57A
(4:53)

Example 57B
(4:56)

Example 58A
(5:03)

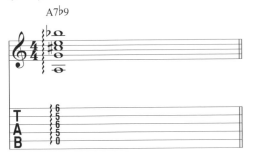

Example 58B
(5:12)

Example 59A
(5:18)

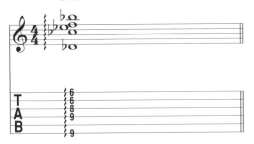

Example 59B
(5:23)

Example 60A
(5:27)

Example 60B
(5:31)

Example 61   Adjacent notes in the chord form provide color
(7:24)

Chapter 7: Bass Lines and Comping

Example 62   **Walking and comping on the I-vi-ii-V**
(:23)

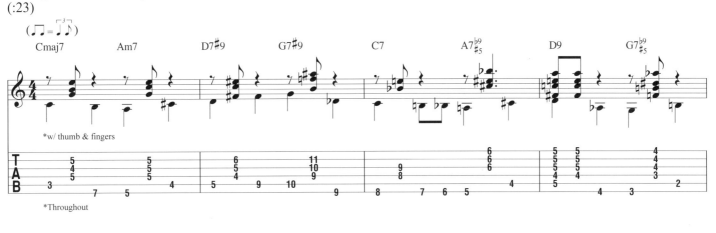

*w/ thumb & fingers

*Throughout

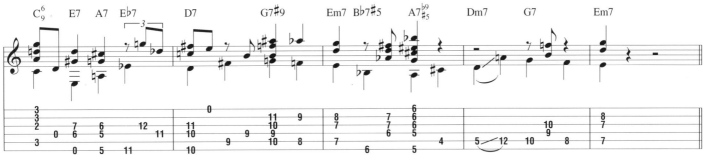

Example 63   **The solid bass line foundation**
(1:10)

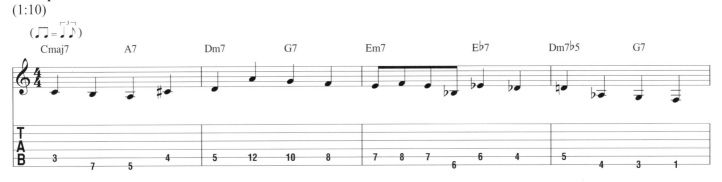

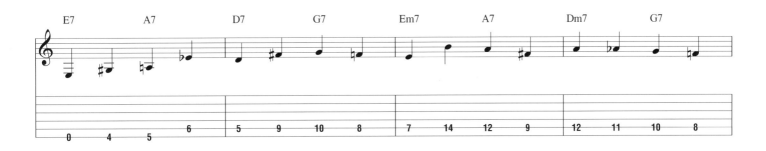

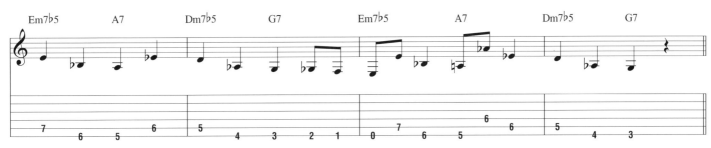

Example 64
(2:09)

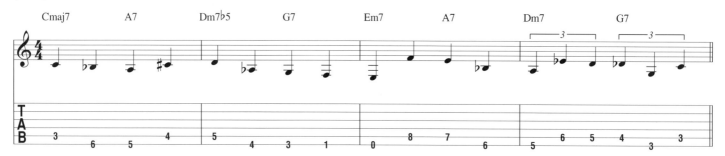

Example 65   The shuffle rhythm
(2:29)

Example 66
(2:32)

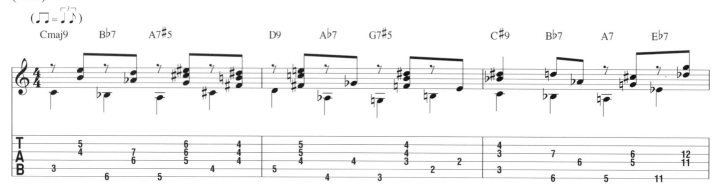

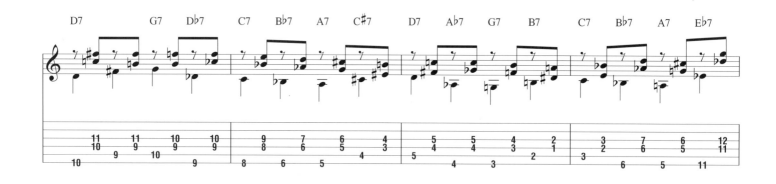

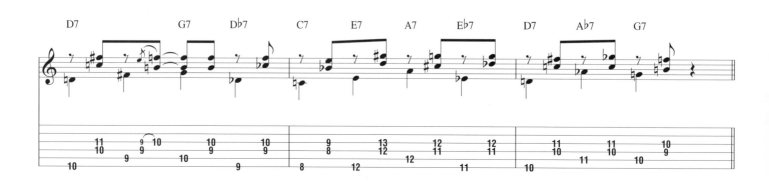

Example 67   Every other accent chord omitted
(3:01)

Example 68
(3:04)

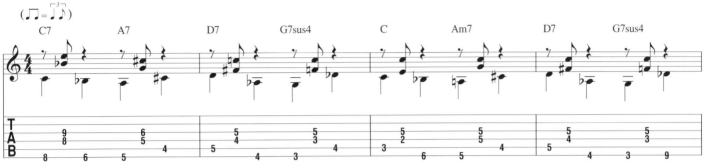

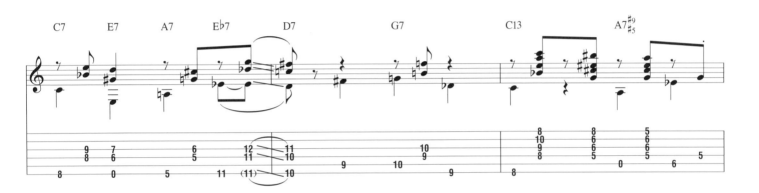

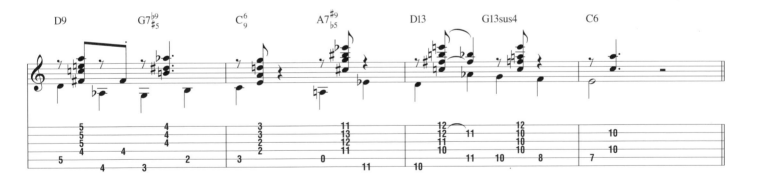

Example 69 **Accents and syncopation**
(4:50)

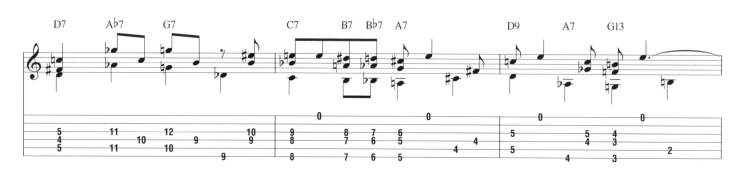

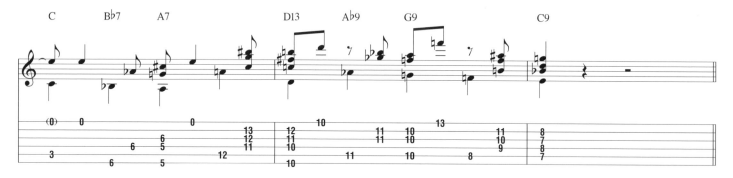

Example 70
(5:36)

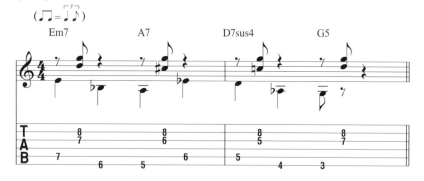

Example 71 **Neutral-sounding notes**
(5:56)

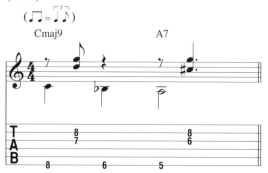

Example 72   Sample with variety

(6:59)

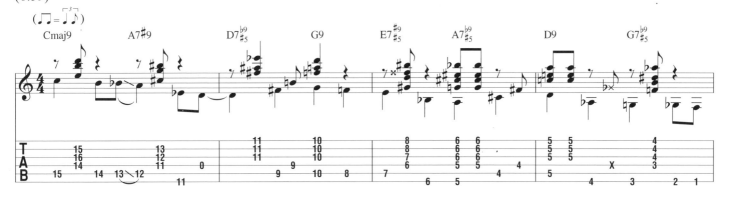

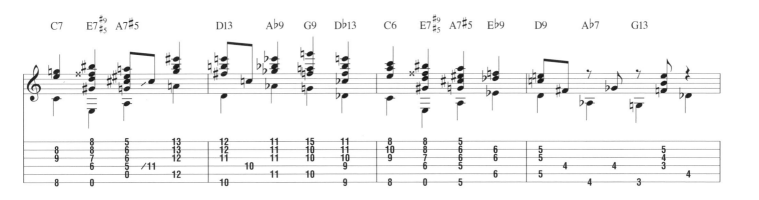

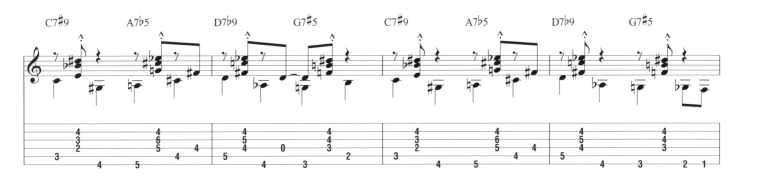

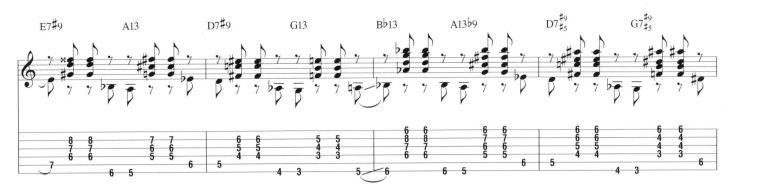

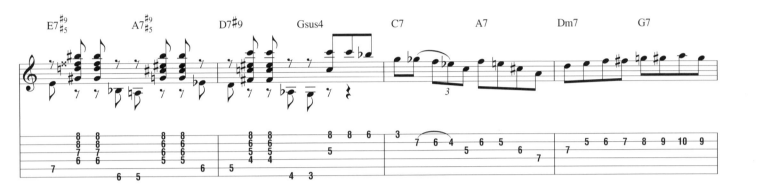

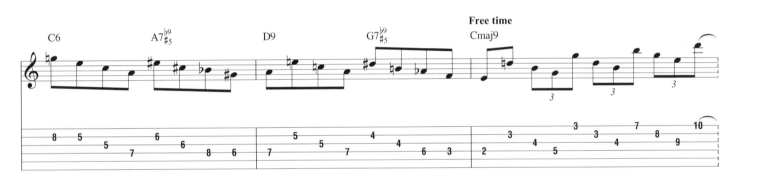

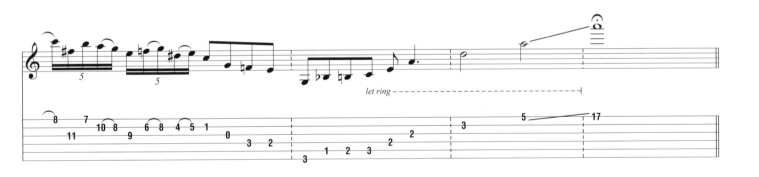

Example 73   Solid foundation: some roots omitted
(8:59)

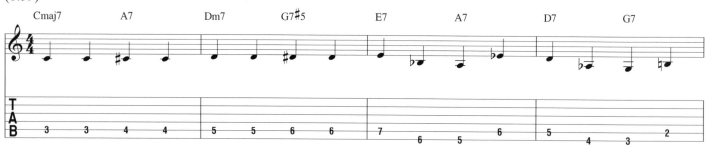

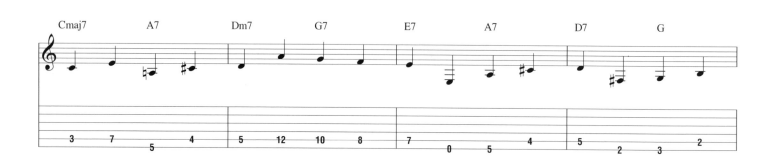

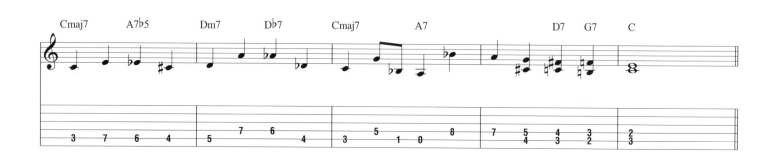

Example 74   Bass line pedal tone
(10:13)

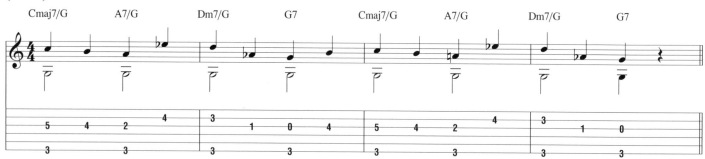

Outro

Example 75   Solo recap
(:04)

GUITAR NOTATION LEGEND

Guitar music can be notated three different ways: on a *musical staff*, in *tablature*, and in *rhythm slashes*.

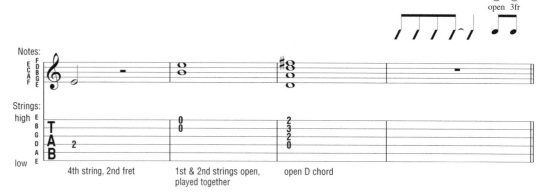

RHYTHM SLASHES are written above the staff. Strum chords in the rhythm indicated. Use the chord diagrams found at the top of the first page of the transcription for the appropriate chord voicings. Round noteheads indicate single notes.

THE MUSICAL STAFF shows pitches and rhythms and is divided by bar lines into measures. Pitches are named after the first seven letters of the alphabet.

TABLATURE graphically represents the guitar fingerboard. Each horizontal line represents a string, and each number represents a fret.

HALF-STEP BEND: Strike the note and bend up 1/2 step.

BEND AND RELEASE: Strike the note and bend up as indicated, then release back to the original note. Only the first note is struck.

HAMMER-ON: Strike the first (lower) note with one finger, then sound the higher note (on the same string) with another finger by fretting it without picking.

TRILL: Very rapidly alternate between the notes indicated by continuously hammering on and pulling off.

PICK SCRAPE: The edge of the pick is rubbed down (or up) the string, producing a scratchy sound.

TREMOLO PICKING: The note is picked as rapidly and continuously as possible.

WHOLE-STEP BEND: Strike the note and bend up one step.

PRE-BEND: Bend the note as indicated, then strike it.

PULL-OFF: Place both fingers on the notes to be sounded. Strike the first note and without picking, pull the finger off to sound the second (lower) note.

TAPPING: Hammer ("tap") the fret indicated with the pick-hand index or middle finger and pull off to the note fretted by the fret hand.

MUFFLED STRINGS: A percussive sound is produced by laying the fret hand across the string(s) without depressing, and striking them with the pick hand.

VIBRATO BAR DIVE AND RETURN: The pitch of the note or chord is dropped a specified number of steps (in rhythm), then returned to the original pitch.

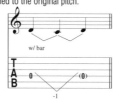

GRACE NOTE BEND: Strike the note and immediately bend up as indicated.

VIBRATO: The string is vibrated by rapidly bending and releasing the note with the fretting hand.

LEGATO SLIDE: Strike the first note and then slide the same fret-hand finger up or down to the second note. The second note is not struck.

NATURAL HARMONIC: Strike the note while the fret-hand lightly touches the string directly over the fret indicated.

PALM MUTING: The note is partially muted by the pick hand lightly touching the string(s) just before the bridge.

VIBRATO BAR SCOOP: Depress the bar just before striking the note, then quickly release the bar.

SLIGHT (MICROTONE) BEND: Strike the note and bend up 1/4 step.

WIDE VIBRATO: The pitch is varied to a greater degree by vibrating with the fretting hand.

SHIFT SLIDE: Same as legato slide, except the second note is struck.

PINCH HARMONIC: The note is fretted normally and a harmonic is produced by adding the edge of the thumb or the tip of the index finger of the pick hand to the normal pick attack.

RAKE: Drag the pick across the strings indicated with a single motion.

VIBRATO BAR DIP: Strike the note and then immediately drop a specified number of steps, then release back to the original pitch.

HOT LICKS

For the first time, the legendary Hot Licks guitar instruction video series is being made available in book format with online access to the classic video footage. All of the guitar tab from the original video booklets has been re-transcribed and edited using modern-day technology to provide you with the most accurate transcriptions ever created for this series. Plus, we've included tab for examples that were previously not transcribed, providing you with the most comprehensive Hot Licks guitar lessons yet. Each book with online video is available for $19.99 each.

Prices, contents, and availability subject to change without notice.

JAZZ GUITAR CHORD
MELODY SOLOS

This series features chord melody arrangements in standard notation and tablature of songs for intermediate guitarists. **INCLUDES TAB**

ALL-TIME STANDARDS

27 songs, including: All of Me • Bewitched • Come Fly with Me • A Fine Romance • Georgia on My Mind • How High the Moon • I'll Never Smile Again • I've Got You Under My Skin • It's De-Lovely • It's Only a Paper Moon • My Romance • Satin Doll • The Surrey with the Fringe on Top • Yesterdays • and more.
00699757 Solo Guitar...................**$15.99**

IRVING BERLIN

27 songs, including: Alexander's Ragtime Band • Always • Blue Skies • Cheek to Cheek • Easter Parade • Happy Holiday • Heat Wave • How Deep Is the Ocean • Puttin' On the Ritz • Remember • They Say It's Wonderful • What'll I Do? • White Christmas • and more.
00700637 Solo Guitar...................**$14.99**

CHRISTMAS CAROLS

26 songs, including: Auld Lang Syne • Away in a Manger • Deck the Hall • God Rest Ye Merry, Gentlemen • Good King Wenceslas • Here We Come A-Wassailing • It Came upon the Midnight Clear • Joy to the World • O Holy Night • O Little Town of Bethlehem • Silent Night • Toyland • We Three Kings of Orient Are • and more.
00701697 Solo Guitar...................**$12.99**

CHRISTMAS JAZZ

21 songs, including Auld Lang Syne • Baby, It's Cold Outside • Cool Yule • Have Yourself a Merry Little Christmas • I've Got My Love to Keep Me Warm • Mary, Did You Know? • Santa Baby • Sleigh Ride • White Christmas • Winter Wonderland • and more.
00171334 Solo Guitar...................**$14.99**

DISNEY SONGS

27 songs, including: Beauty and the Beast • Can You Feel the Love Tonight • Candle on the Water • Colors of the Wind • A Dream Is a Wish Your Heart Makes • Heigh-Ho • Some Day My Prince Will Come • Under the Sea • When You Wish upon a Star • A Whole New World (Aladdin's Theme) • Zip-A-Dee-Doo-Dah • and more.
00701902 Solo Guitar...................**$14.99**

DUKE ELLINGTON

25 songs, including: C-Jam Blues • Caravan • Do Nothin' Till You Hear from Me • Don't Get Around Much Anymore • I Got It Bad and That Ain't Good • I'm Just a Lucky So and So • In a Sentimental Mood • It Don't Mean a Thing (If It Ain't Got That Swing) • Mood Indigo • Perdido • Prelude to a Kiss • Satin Doll • and more.
00700636 Solo Guitar...................**$12.99**

FAVORITE STANDARDS

27 songs, including: All the Way • Autumn in New York • Blue Skies • Cheek to Cheek • Don't Get Around Much Anymore • How Deep Is the Ocean • I'll Be Seeing You • Isn't It Romantic? • It Could Happen to You • The Lady Is a Tramp • Moon River • Speak Low • Take the "A" Train • Willow Weep for Me • Witchcraft • and more.
00699756 Solo Guitar...................**$14.99**

JAZZ BALLADS

27 songs, including: Body and Soul • Darn That Dream • Easy to Love (You'd Be So Easy to Love) • Here's That Rainy Day • In a Sentimental Mood • Misty • My Foolish Heart • My Funny Valentine • The Nearness of You • Stella by Starlight • Time After Time • The Way You Look Tonight • When Sunny Gets Blue • and more.
00699755 Solo Guitar...................**$14.99**

LATIN STANDARDS

27 Latin favorites, including: Água De Beber (Water to Drink) • Desafinado • The Girl from Ipanema • How Insensitive (Insensatez) • Little Boat • Meditation • One Note Samba (Samba De Uma Nota So) • Poinciana • Quiet Nights of Quiet Stars • Samba De Orfeu • So Nice (Summer Samba) • Wave • and more.
00699754 Solo Guitar...................**$14.99**

> "Well-crafted arrangements that sound great and are still accessible to most players."
> – *Guitar Edge* magazine

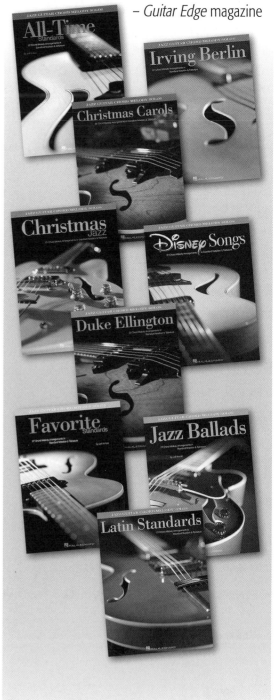

HAL•LEONARD®

Prices, content, and availability subject to change without notice.
Disney Characters and Artwork © Disney Enterprises, Inc.

www.halleonard.com